THE 2013 OKLAHOMA CITY
TORNADOES

THE 2013 OKLAHOMA CITY
TORNADOES

BY STEPHANIE WATSON

CONTENT CONSULTANT
DR. ROBERT J. TRAPP
PURDUE UNIVERSITY
DEPARTMENT OF EARTH, ATMOSPHERIC,
AND PLANETARY SCIENCES

ABDO
Publishing Company

CREDITS

Published by ABDO Publishing Company, PO Box 398166, Minneapolis, MN 55439. Copyright © 2014 by Abdo Consulting Group, Inc. International copyrights reserved in all countries. No part of this book may be reproduced in any form without written permission from the publisher. The Essential Library™ is a trademark and logo of ABDO Publishing Company.

Printed in the United States of America,
North Mankato, Minnesota
102013
012014

 THIS BOOK CONTAINS AT LEAST 10% RECYCLED MATERIALS.

Editor: Karen Latchana Kenney
Series Designer: Becky Daum

Photo credits: Charlie Riedel/AP Images, cover, 2, 40, 44, 60, 66, 92; Sue Ogrocki/ AP Images, 6, 13, 23, 42, 62; Red Line Editorial, 9, 36, 56; Jonathan Ernst/Reuters/ Corbis, 15; Shawn Yorks/The Guymon Daily Herald/AP Images, 16; AP Images, 20; Tony Gutierrez/AP Images, 24, 84; Gene Blevins/Corbis, 28; National Oceanic and Atmospheric Administration, 31; Corbis, 32; iStock/Thinkstock, 36 (inset); Steve Sisney/AP Images, 39; U.S. Air Force, Staff Sgt. Jonathan Snyder/AP Images, 47; James Breeden/Corbis, 51; Kim Johnson Flodin/AP Images, 52; J. Pat Carter, Tony Gutierrez/ AP Images, 59; Steve Sisney/AP Images, 70; Chris Machian/AP Images, 72, 76, 79; Marion Cunningham/Discovery Channel/AP Images, 82; Charlie Riedel/Corbis, 87

Library of Congress Control Number: 2013946961

Cataloging-in-Publication Data

Watson, Stephanie, 1969-
The 2013 Oklahoma City tornadoes / Stephanie Watson.
  p. cm. -- (Essential events)
Includes bibliographical references and index.
ISBN 978-1-62403-257-8
1. Tornadoes--Juvenile literature. 2. Tornadoes--Oklahoma--Oklahoma City--2013--Juvenile literature. 3. Natural disasters--Juvenile literature. I. Title.
551.55--dc23

2013946961

CONTENTS

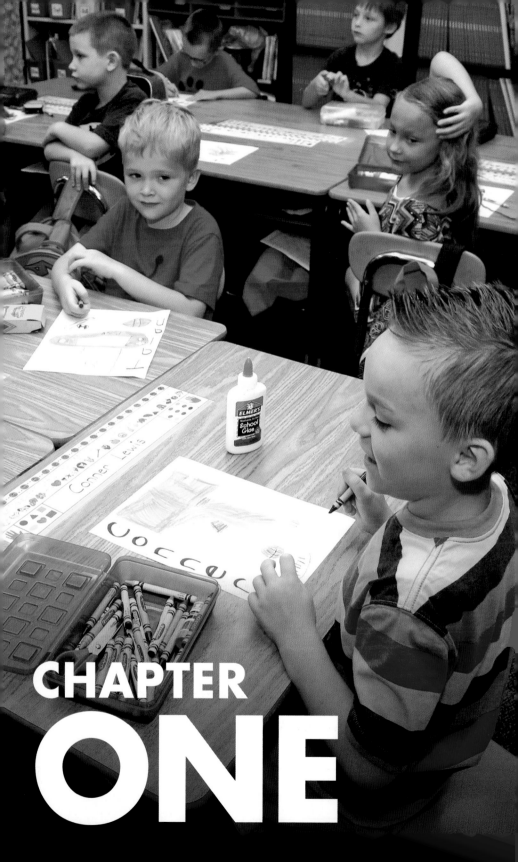

CHAPTER
ONE

TAKING COVER

At 2:45 p.m. on May 20, 2013, the students at Plaza Towers Elementary School in Moore, Oklahoma, were nearing the end of their school day. On that muggy Monday afternoon, the children were not packing up their backpacks to head home. They were preparing for a major storm to hit.

Starting that morning, Oklahoma weather forecasters predicted that a line of severe, tornado-producing storms was going to roll through the Oklahoma City area. They warned residents to be alert and take shelter if necessary. At 2:40 p.m., Oklahoma City sounded Moore's tornado sirens. Everyone in town knew the sirens meant a tornado was imminent. Twenty minutes later, the weather service issued a tornado emergency—the strongest possible tornado warning. This was not just any tornado. A massive and extremely dangerous storm was on its way.

Moore is a suburb approximately ten miles (16 km) south of Oklahoma City. Moore's 57,000 residents

Students of Plaza Towers Elementary School witnessed the destructive force of the tornadoes that hit their city and school on May 20, 2013.

were used to tornadoes. This suburb sits in the heart of Tornado Alley, an area in the central United States that is known as one of the most tornado-prone parts of the country.

When the sirens started ringing on the afternoon of May 20, the teachers at Plaza Towers Elementary followed the school's tornado emergency plans. Teachers filed the children out of their classrooms and into the hallways, where they would be away from windows that could shatter and outside walls that could crumble. Ideally schoolchildren are taken into safe rooms during

TORNADO ALLEY

In the United States, two regions are known for the large number of tornadoes that strike them each year. One region is Florida. The other region is called Tornado Alley. It is a strip of land that includes most of Kansas, Nebraska, Oklahoma, and South Dakota, and parts of Texas, Colorado, Minnesota, Iowa, Missouri, and New Mexico.

In 1952, the US Air Force's Severe Weather Warning Center created a project to study tornadoes in the storm-prone area stretching from Texas to Colorado and Nebraska. They called the project Tornado Alley. The first time the public saw the name was in a May 5, 1957, *New York Times* article calling the area "the incubator of nature's deadliest storms."[1]

Tornado Alley may be home to the most intense and greatest number of tornadoes, but it does not have a monopoly on the deadliest tornadoes. Three states outside Tornado Alley—Mississippi, Alabama, and Arkansas—have some of the highest numbers of tornado deaths. This area has been nicknamed Dixie Alley.

Tornado Alley

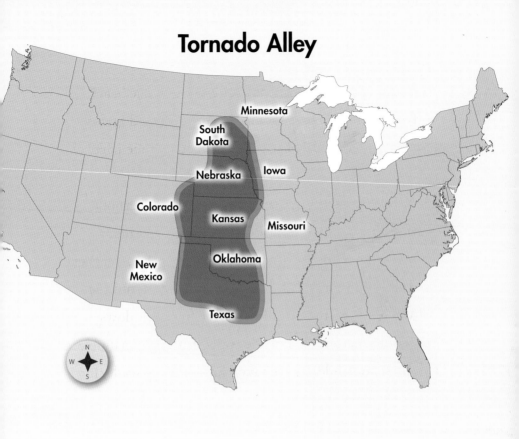

severe storms. These rooms are inside shelters able to withstand tornado-force winds. However, Plaza Towers Elementary was not built with safe rooms.

The children knew just what to do during tornado drills. They had to march into the hallway, crouch down, and cover their heads and necks. But that day, it was not a drill. A voice over the intercom yelled for them to take cover. The children did not know it, but an EF5 tornado—the most powerful kind of tornado in existence—was headed straight for the school.

Finding Shelter

While the students huddled in the school's hallways, others in the Moore area also rushed to find shelter. Teachers at other local schools—including Briarwood Elementary School and the Agapeland Learning Center—tried to protect the children in their care. In homes around town, residents ran to find safe spots to hide.

Rebecca Garland and her husband, Dan, were in their home when they heard the storm warning. They quickly ran from their home on SW 149th street in south Oklahoma City to get Dan's 91-year-old mother, who lived next door. Together, they went to the storm cellar they had built alongside their home in 2001, after the last major tornado hit Moore. The Garlands, along with a few of their neighbors, climbed down the metal ladder into the tiny cellar. They slammed the door shut just as the tornado began whirling toward them.

Tonya Williams, a 38-year-old mother, did not have a storm cellar. She hid inside a hall closet in her home, along with her two young children and their three dogs. Williams put bicycle helmets on her children to protect them from flying debris. She lay on top of them, using her body as a shield. Then Williams began to pray.

In a home near Moore's movie theater, Mark Ellerd was working in his garage when he heard on the radio that a tornado was headed straight for the theater. "I could actually hear the roar of it coming from the southwest," he said.[3] He grabbed his cocker spaniel, Molly, and hid from the storm in his bedroom closet.

Lando Hite rushed to the stables at the Orr Family Farm, where he worked as a horse caretaker. He freed as many horses as he could, giving them a chance to run away from the storm. By the time he was done, there was no time left for him to find a basement or shelter.

> "We had gotten in our hall closet, and we heard the train sound and doors started to open. The next thing you know, everything was pushed in on us, and the house was completely gone."[4]
> —Tonya Williams, tornado survivor

He hunkered down in one of the horse's stalls and hoped for the best.

Life-or-Death Decisions

When the tornado sirens rang, many people in Moore had to make a life-or-death decision: Should they stay where they were or try to outrun the storm? Parents made the wrenching choice of whether to pick up their children at school or leave them there to ride out the storm. "I've always said the worst scenario is school is in session and the tornado approaches or develops," says Gary England, a then forecaster at Oklahoma television station KWTV-9. "The mothers and dads hear the warning, see the warning and they jump in their cars and head for the schools. You can't imagine the fear that they had."[5]

Patrick Smith was one of the parents who decided to pick up his children from school. They rushed home, trying to beat the storm but barely staying ahead of it. "The tornado seemed to chase me all the way," he said. Once home, Smith had just enough time to put his two kids into the bathtub and cover them with a mattress. As the storm barreled down on them, he yelled, "I love you."[6]

Leaving their kids at school was the safer choice for some, whose homes were gone after the storm.

Angie Tennyson rushed to her children's school when she heard of the tornado warning. "I got there within an hour," she said. "And people look at you funny when you take these warnings that seriously. But I'm glad I did. We made it into the shelter with just minutes to spare."[7]

Carrie Long, a parent of two teens in the Moore school system, decided to leave her children at their schools. For her family, it was the right decision. Her home was completely destroyed by the tornado. She said, "If I'd gotten my kids out and taken them home, they'd be dead. There's just nothing left of our home."[8]

The Storm Approaches

Back at Plaza Towers Elementary, first-grade teacher Becky Evans huddled in a hallway with her students.

The children crouched against the walls, covering their heads and necks with their hands.

The tornado spun ever closer. One of the school's skylights shattered, and the wall where Evans's students were crouching started crumbling. Evans quickly pulled her students into a nearby bathroom. Sixth-grade teacher Rhonda Crosswhite did the only thing she could think to do to protect the six students in her care—she lay on top of them. A little boy pleaded with her, "I love you, I love you, please don't die with me."[9]

Another sixth-grade teacher, Janice Brim, ushered her students into a hall closet that was only five feet (1.5 m) wide. "I remember their terrified eyes, looking at me for hope," she said. "They wanted me to promise them that we'd be okay, but I couldn't bring myself to make that promise."[10]

The citizens of Moore hid and waited. At 3:16 p.m., their world turned upside down.

US President Barack Obama hugs the teachers and first responders who saved Plaza Towers' students' lives during his visit on May 26, 2013.

CHAPTER
TWO

THE APPROACHING STORM

E very spring, three competing air masses come together over Oklahoma and the rest of Tornado Alley. These masses set the stage for tornadoes. Warm, humid air travels north from the Gulf of Mexico. It runs head-on into cold air riding the jet stream that travels down from Canada. Joining them is a mass of hot, dry air from the Southwest. As these contending air masses collide, they make the weather very unstable. Conditions become ideal for severe thunderstorms to form.

By May, the 2013 tornado season was unusually quiet. In fact, it was the first time the United States had not had a single EF1 or stronger tornado strike during the month of May. Typically tornadoes start forming in the Great Plains and the Midwest by March or April. Oklahoma had a cool spring so far that year. The weather had been unusually quiet for the area.

Severe weather is common in Oklahoma during the spring.

THE ENHANCED FUJITA TORNADO SCALE

Tornadoes are measured on the Enhanced Fujita (EF) scale from EF0 to EF5. Meteorologists use the scale to rate a tornado's severity based on how much damage it causes.

EF	WIND SPEEDS	DAMAGE
EF0	65–85 mph (104–137 kmh)	Peels roofs, breaks branches off trees
EF1	86–110 mph (138–177 kmh)	Strips roofs, overturns mobile homes, tears off outside doors, breaks windows
EF2	111–135 mph (179–217 kmh)	Tears off roofs, moves home foundations, destroys mobile homes, snaps large trees, lifts cars off the ground
EF3	136–165 mph (219–265 kmh)	Destroys whole stories of homes, peels bark off trees, lifts large cars off the ground and throws them, blows away weak buildings
EF4	166–200 mph (267–322 kmh)	Levels whole houses, throws cars
EF5	More than 200 mph (322 kmh)	Tears homes from their foundations, makes cars fly through the air like missiles

mph=miles per hour
kmh=kilometers per hour

Ingredients of a Storm

As Monday, May 20, dawned, the Oklahoma City area was warm and muggy. All of the ingredients were in place for a tornado. An influx of air from the

Gulf of Mexico made the atmosphere hot and moist. Temperatures rose from 70 degrees Fahrenheit (21°C) to more than 80 degrees Fahrenheit (27°C).

There were strong jet-stream winds at high levels of the atmosphere, as well as wind shear—changing wind speeds and directions at different heights. There were also strong winds—52 to 57 miles per hour (84 to 92 kmh) in the lower levels of the atmosphere. They pushed the warm and cool air masses together, forming thunderstorms.

Tracking the Storm

When meteorologist Rick Smith got to work at 7:00 a.m. on May 20, he knew it was going to be a busy

THE BIRTH OF A TORNADO

To make a tornado, the right weather ingredients have to be in place. There must be warm, moist air in the lower part of the atmosphere and cold, dry air in the upper atmosphere. This combination is an unstable mixture of air, and if it is disturbed by a frontal system, a thunderstorm can be triggered. Most tornadoes form from supercell thunderstorms—storms with rotating strong currents of air called updrafts. A tornado forms when the wind is strong and blows in different directions at multiple speeds and various heights of the atmosphere. As air rises from the ground into the storm, a horizontal tube of spinning air forms. A strong updraft can make the horizontal tube of spinning air become vertical, forming a spinning funnel. As the wind rotates more tightly and lowers, the tornado funnel touches the ground and begins its path of destruction.

Meteorologist Rick Smith saw the signs of a major storm in Moore on May 20, 2013.

day. Smith is a warning coordinator for the NWS office in Norman, Oklahoma. At his workstation, he checked the radar systems and satellite images. He called the weather he saw brewing "A classic Oklahoma storm situation."[1]

Meteorologists know when a storm is about to form and where it will hit because they constantly monitor the skies. The NWS has satellites in space, which can show storm patterns. It also has 155 Doppler radar systems on the ground.[2] These systems use radio waves to find areas of rain and hail in the clouds.

It might seem strange that a warm-weather storm could produce chunks of ice, but hail is common with severe thunderstorms. Inside the thunderstorm are updrafts of warm air and downdrafts of cold air. Sometimes water droplets get carried in an updraft to levels in the atmosphere where the temperature is well below 32 degrees Fahrenheit (0°C). The cold air makes the water freeze.

The now-frozen water droplets can be carried up into the frigid air over and over again, increasing their size by adding layer after layer of ice. Eventually, the ice falls back to Earth as hail. Hailstones can range from the size of a pea to the size of a baseball. Considering hail can travel at speeds reaching 120 miles per hour (193 kmh), it can cause a great deal of damage when it reaches the ground.

DOPPLER RADAR

Doppler radar is a technology that helps meteorologists track storms. It can determine how far away and how strong a storm is by sending out bursts of radio waves. The process is super fast—each burst lasts for only approximately 0.00000157 seconds. The radar calculates the storm's distance by recording how long it takes the radio waves to reach the raindrops or hailstones, bounce off them, and return to the radar's antenna. This process creates a signal meteorologists can analyze to determine the intensity of the storm. A stronger signal indicates a more intense storm.

A Turbulent Start

It had been a turbulent start to the week. Just the day before, a line of tornadoes tore through Kansas, Oklahoma, and Iowa. One of the tornadoes measured an EF4—the second-most-powerful type of tornado in existence. The storms, which also produced baseball-sized hail and heavy rain, destroyed homes, injured dozens of people, and killed two people near Shawnee, Oklahoma.

As Smith looked at his radar screen, he noted weather conditions looked even more dangerous than they had the previous day. "It was apparent that it was going to be very bad. About as bad as it gets," he said.[3]

The radar image changed from a few clouds to a severe storm very quickly. "It went from being a benign-looking blip to a supercell in 10 to 15 minutes," said researcher Robin Tanamachi. She was watching the storm from her post at the National Severe Storms

Storm chasers take photos and measure wind speeds of approaching storms.

Laboratory in Norman, Oklahoma. "All the ingredients were there at the right time."[5]

Severe storm researchers were not the only people with their eyes on the skies. Professional and amateur tornado spotters drove the roads around Oklahoma City, watching the clouds form. They called, texted, and e-mailed their reports to Smith and other meteorologists at the NWS. Television station crews also were on the ground. From the data coming in, it soon became clear a deadly storm was bearing down on the town of Moore in the suburbs of Oklahoma City. Meteorologists knew it was time to get the word out to local residents.

CHAPTER
THREE

TORNADO SIRENS WAIL

Between 2:20 and 2:30 p.m., the NWS issued a severe thunderstorm warning for the Oklahoma City area. This meant incoming storms might be strong enough to produce tornadoes. At 2:40 p.m., the NWS upgraded to a tornado warning. A tornado had formed or was indicated on Doppler radar. Tornado sirens across Moore began wailing. The NWS also issued a weather advisory on television and the Internet, urging residents to "take cover now in a storm shelter or an interior room of a sturdy building. Stay away from doors and windows."[1]

Living in the heart of Tornado Alley, tornado warnings were common for the residents of Moore. "As much as any place on earth, folks who live in Moore know what severe weather alerts mean," said Bill Bunting, chief of operations for the NWS Storm Prediction Center (SPC) in Norman.[2]

Storm clouds moved through the sky above Moore on the day of the storm.

Because severe storms are so common in that part of the country and most of them do not produce tornadoes, people who live in the Oklahoma City area sometimes fail to take the warnings seriously. "There's always talk about tornadoes," said high school student Brandon Garrison. "I honestly didn't think it would be that big a deal."[3]

The Tornado Forms

Within ten minutes after the tornado sirens started wailing, a funnel cloud formed over Newcastle, a town approximately 12 miles (19 km) southwest of Moore. By 2:56 p.m., the funnel started descending from the sky.

Within a couple of minutes, the tornado touched down. It spun northeast, picking up debris and growing larger and larger as it churned across the land. The tornado swirled on a northeasterly track. It headed straight for the city of Moore.

A Wall of Dark Clouds

In Moore, the sky turned dark. The gentle breeze from earlier that morning turned into a sharp wind. Hail fell with loud plunks, pelting the ground. Weather conditions quickly deteriorated.

At 3:01 p.m., the NWS issued a tornado emergency for the city of Moore and the southern part of Oklahoma City. A tornado emergency is the strongest-possible tornado warning. People had just minutes to prepare before a twister of epic proportions would be right on top of them.

Meanwhile, a flurry of e-mails, text messages, and other warnings flooded the Internet. Through Twitter, the NWS tried to get its message to as many people as it could.

STORM DEBRIS

Tornadoes collect a variety of debris, which can range from an object as small as a photograph to one as large as a semitrailer. And tornadoes can carry debris a long way. A tornado that struck Kansas and Nebraska in April 1911 picked up a check and deposited it 223 miles (359 km) away. In 1930, a person was blown a full mile (1.6 km). The May 22, 2011, tornado that hit Joplin, Missouri, lifted more than 15,000 vehicles and tossed them as far as several blocks away.[4] Some people in the town were never able to find their cars.

NOAA mobile Doppler radar units track deadly storms.

It posted, "The tornado is so large you may not realize it's a tornado. If you are in Moore, go to shelter NOW!"[5] The tornado had become embedded inside a larger cloud. It had grown so huge it looked like a solid wall of dark clouds. The tornado funnel was almost impossible to see inside the cloud wall.

On every local television network, meteorologists issued dire warnings to people in the massive tornado's path. "You folks in Moore, you need to grab whatever

TORNADO EMERGENCY

Not all storm warnings are the same. Often the first warning issued is a severe thunderstorm watch. It means conditions are right for a severe thunderstorm—with hail and strong winds. The next level up is a severe thunderstorm warning. It is issued when a storm is about to form or has formed.

Tornado watches are issued when conditions are prime for a tornado to develop. Tornado warnings are sent out when a tornado or funnel cloud has been spotted or indicated on Doppler radar. Both are common in Oklahoma. Yet the term *tornado emergency* is used in only very special circumstances.

The term *tornado emergency* was created after an EF5 tornado struck the Moore area on May 3, 1999. Meteorologist David Andra of the NWS came up with the name to warn people a really serious tornado was on its way. Issuing a tornado emergency told residents in the path of the storm, "This is different; this is deadly," said NWS meteorologist Rick Smith. "It came up in a moment of inspiration, but it was very effective. People understood it." Meteorologists rarely used the tornado emergency warning until the May 20 storm. "Seeing what we saw on TV and knowing what was happening, it was an easy decision to use it again," Smith added.[6]

THE TORNADO FROM SPACE

One of several weather satellites in space took video of the massive storm on May 20, 2013. The NWS uses the GOES satellite system to help monitor and forecast the weather. On the satellite video, a swirling mass of clouds could be seen. The GOES-13 gave weather forecasters updated images of the storm system every 15 minutes, which helped them issue warnings to the public.

it is you need to grab and you need to go underground," KFOR chief meteorologist Mike Morgan urged viewers as he showed them the radar image of the violent storms headed their way. On the image was a mass of red and yellow, indicating the most intense kind of storm. Morgan's warnings became more urgent. "You can't think, you can't delay. You've got to act . . . act to save your life and save your loved one's lives."[7]

In total, the city of Moore sounded its tornado sirens three times. Then the twister was upon the city.

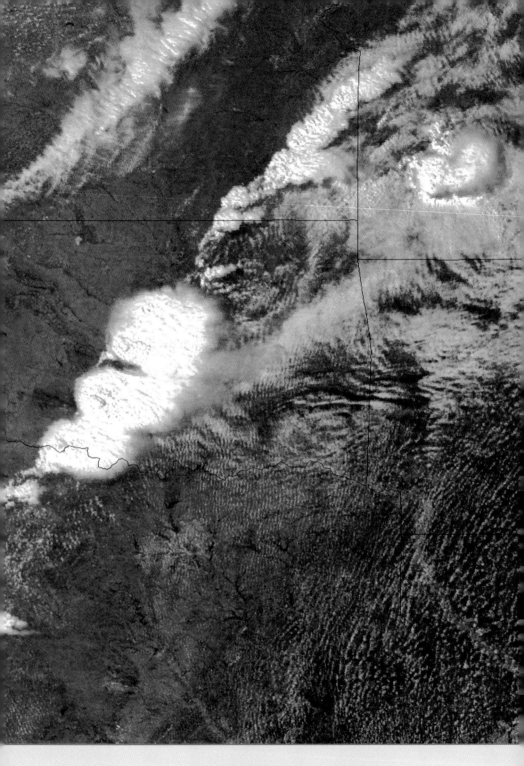

The NOAA GOES-13 satellite showed the
storms from space on May 20, 2013.

CHAPTER FOUR

IN THE TORNADO'S PATH

A meteorologist at KFOR television called the storm about to hit Moore "the worst tornado in the history of the world."[1] His words might have been an overstatement, but few could match this tornado for its combination of size, strength, and length of time on the ground.

The Moore tornado measured more than one mile (1.6 km) across—the length of more than 20 football fields. At first, meteorologists thought it was an EF4 tornado. Later they upgraded it to an EF5. Its wind speeds were estimated to reach up to 200 miles per hour (320 kmh).[2]

Caught in the Storm

At 3:16 p.m., the tornado entered Moore. For anyone in its 14-mile (22.5 km) path, the next few minutes were absolutely terrifying. The tornado's winds tore

Michael Welch of Blanchard, Oklahoma, took a video of the approaching funnel on May 20, 2013.

through everything in its way. The tornado was loud, too. "It sounded like a jet plane and a freight train roaring together," one postal worker said.[3]

The tornado lifted houses off their foundations and shredded walls into splinters. Cars flew through the air and signposts and power lines hurled through the sky at great speeds. Any objects in the tornado's path were completely obliterated.

In Moore's schools, children hid from the swirling winds in closets, bathrooms, and hallways. They cried, shook, and feared for their lives as the walls around them crumbled. At the Agapeland Learning Center, workers cowered in the bathrooms with more than a dozen young children. They sang "You Are My Sunshine" and other songs to keep the kids calm. Their words could barely be heard above the roar of the storm.

The scene was just as chaotic at Highland East Junior High School. "The room started shaking.

And we heard things crashing into the building. We heard glass shattering," said 14-year-old Lanie Wolfe, a seventh-grade student.[5] Meanwhile, Lanie's mother texted her frantically, trying to make sure she was okay. Caught up in the middle of the storm, Lanie could not reply.

Parents all over town panicked. The few minutes the tornado was on the ground seemed like hours. Amy Selix was at work 15 miles (24 km) away from Moore

THE MOST EXPENSIVE TORNADOES IN HISTORY

Early estimates of the tornado that struck Moore, Oklahoma, put the property damage in the range of $2 billion.[6] Once all the damage is tallied, it could prove to be the most expensive tornado in history. Here is NOAA's list of some of the most expensive tornadoes ever to hit the United States.

SAINT LOUIS, MISSOURI, ON MAY 27, 1896
Cost: $12 million ($2.6 billion in 2011 dollars)
This tornado damaged or destroyed more than 8,000 buildings and killed more than 250 people.[7]

TRI-STATE TORNADO, ON MARCH 18, 1925
Cost: $16 million ($1.46 billion in 2011 dollars)
The Tri-State Tornado tracked 219 miles (352 km) across Illinois, Indiana, and Missouri.[8]

SAINT LOUIS, MISSOURI, ON SEPTEMBER 29, 1927
Cost: $22 million ($2.7 billion in 2011 dollars)
This tornado tore a seven-mile (11.3-km) path of destruction through the middle of Saint Louis.[9]

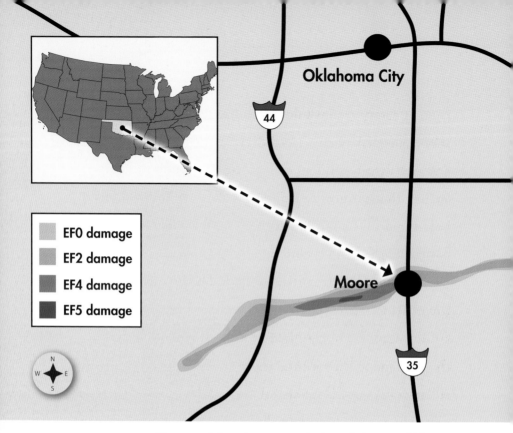

EF0 damage
EF2 damage
EF4 damage
EF5 damage

Oklahoma City

44

Moore

35

The tornado's path tore straight through the city of Moore.

when the tornado touched down. Her five-year-old son, Xander, and 22-month-old daughter, Edie, were at school and day care in Moore. "It was simply terrifying, watching the storm and seeing it form," she said. "I just stood there, frozen, with my hands on my face. I felt physically sick."[10]

Chaos . . . and Then Silence

In their storm cellar, the Garland family and a few neighbors hid from the storm. The tornado was so powerful even being underground did not completely protect them. The whole cellar shook furiously. Dan Garland and two other men fought against the ferocious winds to hold the door shut. They were barely able to keep it closed.

In another storm cellar in town, Ricky Stover and his family were just as terrified as the Garlands. They locked their cellar door, but the powerful winds blew the latch open. "It ripped open the door. Glass and debris started slamming on us." They watched as the winds tore apart their neighbor's house and blew it away. "We thought we were dead," Stover said.[11]

From the stables at the Orr Family Farm, Lando Hite saw "horses and stuff flying around everywhere," he said.[12] People in the storm's path had just one hope—that the storm

TORNADOES: MOVIE VERSUS REALITY

The 1996 blockbuster movie *Twister* stars actors Helen Hunt and Bill Paxton as storm chasers caught up in a massive tornado outbreak. As they chased the storms, they found themselves right in the middle of not one but several tornadoes. The special effects in the movie were some of the best to date, and the movie did very well at the box office. But meteorologists had some issues with the way tornadoes were portrayed in the film.

In the movie, tornadoes dropped down from nearly clear skies. In reality, tornadoes form out of supercell thunderstorms. In the movie, the funnel clouds hopped back and forth, skipping across fields and roads almost as though they were chasing the storm chasers. In the real world, tornadoes follow fairly straight paths.

would spare their lives. They protected themselves as best they could. Some people prayed. And they waited through those terrible minutes as the storm ripped through town.

Finally, at 3:36 p.m., approximately 40 minutes after the funnel first touched down, it lifted up into the sky near Lake Stanley Draper—ten miles (16 km) east of Moore. The city of Moore sat in stunned silence.

Rescuers later found a horse in the remains
of barns and a day care center.

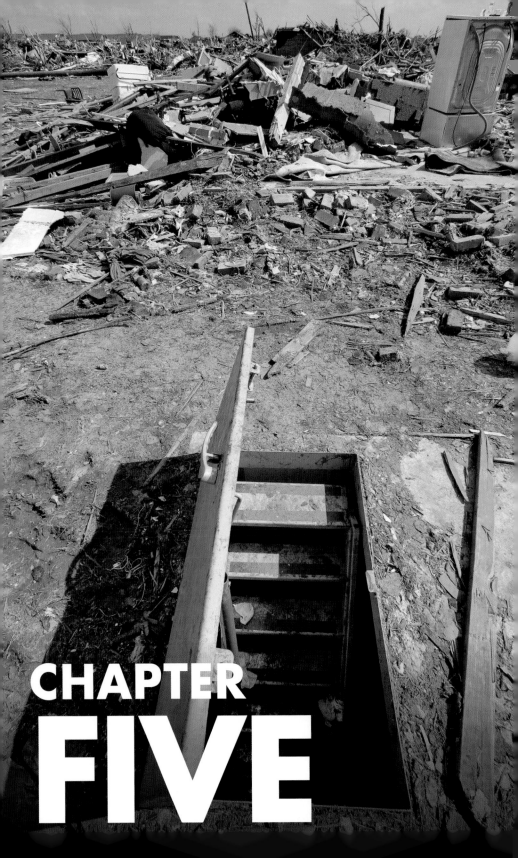

CHAPTER
FIVE

AFTER THE STORM

The tornado retreated to the sky after its trek through the Oklahoma City suburbs. On its journey, the tornado spun across the rural town of Newcastle, barreled through the densely populated suburb of Moore, and crossed two interstate highways and a river before finally petering out in the recreational area of Lake Stanley Draper.

As it rose, the funnel cloud let go of the debris it had collected. Pieces of homes and businesses crashed to the ground. Family pictures, children's bicycles, and countless mementos of residents' lives lay scattered in pieces.

After the whoosh and roar of the tornado's winds, quiet returned. And the people of Moore and southern Oklahoma City emerged from their hiding places— closets, bathtubs, basements, and storm shelters—to survey the damage.

The people of Moore emerged from their shelters to find the destruction caused by the tornado.

A woman carries her child away from the wreckage
of Plaza Towers Elementary School.

People Emerge

Kelly Byrne, a mother who had ridden out the storm
with her two young daughters in a neighbor's storm
shelter, climbed out into the world. What she saw was
complete devastation. Her neighborhood was in ruins.
A car that had been parked in her driveway was on its
side in front of her house. Her attic was inside the garage
and a recliner sat in her hot tub. Despite the magnitude

of the damage, she realized she was lucky to be alive. "When there are cars flying through the air, and trees and parts of houses, there's only so much you can do to hide from it," she said.[1]

Tonya Williams and her two children were still in the closet of their home. The roof and top floor had fallen down, trapping them inside. Neighbors were able to pull them from the wreckage of their house. They survived with only minor injuries.

Tiffany Thronesberry's mother was also lucky. She called out to her daughter in a panic after the tornado passed. She yelled, "Help me, help me! I can't breathe! The house is on top of me!"[2] Neighbors pulled her out with just a few scratches and bruises.

Many residents of Moore and the southern part of Oklahoma City lost everything they owned. Luis Lopez pointed

DIFFERENCES IN DAMAGE

Tornadoes can be especially frightening because of their random path of destruction. The Oklahoma tornado destroyed Rebecca Garland's home, but not far up the road, Marlene Moan's house was barely touched. The only damage was to her roof and garage door.

Meteorologists say the reason for the differences in damage is likely because of the way buildings are constructed. Stronger homes are more likely to survive a tornado than weaker ones. Also, some homes are protected by their location—sheltered against the tornado's winds by other homes or structures.

Plaza Towers Elementary School lay in pieces after the tornado passed.

reporters to a pile of bricks. "That was my house," he said. "It's gone."[3] His sport-utility vehicle had blown 50 yards (46 m) away from the house.

When Rebecca Garland stuck her head out of her storm cellar, her street looked like a war zone. There were downed trees and twisted pieces of metal everywhere. A boat sat on top of a house. Garland's house was gone. So was her mother-in-law's home. But they realized how lucky they were. "It's just stuff, you know, and I'm thinking of the little kids at school and their parents," she said.[4]

Plaza Towers Elementary School

After the storm had passed, teachers and students who had been hiding in Plaza Towers Elementary School looked up. The roof was gone, and the building had been reduced to rubble.

Because of the actions of teachers who had sheltered students and covered them with their own bodies, most of the children were safe. But seven of the children had not survived. They had been trapped in water and drowned but nobody knew why.

Parents of the children at Plaza Towers Elementary, Briarwood Elementary, and other damaged schools in the area were terrified when they saw video of the schools on television. They feared the worst might have happened to their own children. Many of them walked for miles, through a dangerous sea of downed power lines, open gas lines, tree limbs, and destroyed buildings, to find their children. Most of the parents were eventually reunited with their children. "They were out of

"Today was the day that no parent wants to encounter, the words you never want to hear as a parent. . . . Our baby didn't make it."[5]
—Kristen Conatzer, mother of nine-year-old tornado victim Emily, written on her Facebook page

breath and crying but just so happy to see them," one teacher said.[6]

It took Melissa Rodriguez's mother all day to find her daughter at a local hospital. The nine-year-old had been pulled out from under a collapsed wall. Miraculously, she survived with only bruises.

Joshua Hornsby was driving to pick up his nine-year-old daughter, Janae, when the storm hit. He got stuck in traffic and did not arrive until the tornado had already destroyed Plaza Towers Elementary. "I had to park around the corner from the school," he said. "And when I hit the corner so where I could see the school, the school was gone. My heart just sank."[7] Janae was among the seven student victims of the school.

Victims of the Storm

Twenty-four people died during the tornado.[8] The oldest victim was 65—a retired General Motors employee named Hemant Bhonde. He lived across the street from Plaza Towers Elementary School.

ANIMAL VICTIMS

Hundreds of cats, dogs, and other animals died in the twister. In June, a group of families held a memorial service for their pets at the Orr Family Farm in Moore. "It's a labor of love when you work with animals, and they were pretty special," said farm owner Glen Orr.[9] He choked back tears at the loss of dozens of his own horses.

National Guard members help Elise Hopkins
search through the rubble of her home.

The youngest victim, Case Futrell, was just four months
old. He was hiding with his mother, Megan, in the walk-
in cooler at a 7-Eleven store when the storm hit and the
roof collapsed on them.

Another one of the storm's young victims, Kyle
Davis, was a third grader at Plaza Towers. He loved
monster trucks and playing soccer. Kyle's parents called
him "Hammy" because he always hammed it up—acting
silly in front of others.

The Devastation Outside

In addition to the loss of life, the tornado injured more than 375 people and destroyed approximately 12,000 homes.[10] Neighborhoods that were once filled with houses and families were flattened.

For the next few days, rescuers—including dozens of National Guard members with specially trained search-and-rescue dogs and volunteers who traveled from all over the country—combed the rubble. They were trying to find anyone who might still be trapped inside homes, schools, and businesses. Local hospitals

LOOKING FOR GYPSY

The Satterlee family adopted their cat, Gypsy, not long after moving into their home in Moore. When the tornado hit, destroying their house, they thought they had lost Gypsy forever.

But Misty Satterlee was not ready to give up hope of finding her beloved pet. "There's a tiny part of me that just wanted to hang on and keep looking for her because she's our family," she said. "We've had her eight years, and she's part of us, and we weren't complete without her."

Three weeks after the storm hit, Satterlee was combing through the rubble of her home, and she decided to call for Gypsy one last time. In response, she heard a tiny "meow." Satterlee and some neighbors knocked a hole in a wall and found Gypsy. The cat was skinny and shaken but still alive. Moore firefighters pulled Gypsy out of the wall, and she was treated at a local veterinarian's office. "I'm so happy to have her back, our family's complete now," Satterlee said.[11]

and medical centers were bombarded with patients who had broken bones, cuts, and other injuries. Moore Medical Center was also damaged by the tornado. More than a dozen parked cars were thrown against the front of the building. All of the patients and staff were able to get to a safe zone in the middle of the building before the storm hit.

There were also amazing survival stories. Ninia Lay's house was flattened with her still inside the closet. She was trapped for two hours after the storm. Yet rescuers finally found her and dug her out.

Briarwood Elementary School was completely destroyed by the tornado. Yet all of the children emerged. Only a few had minor injuries. Agapeland Learning Center was flattened, but all of the children inside survived.

Some people made incredible discoveries among the rubble. While digging through the pile of debris that had once been his house, Tom Bridges found an envelope containing $2,000 he had left on top of a windowsill. Don Jackson spotted his wife's wedding ring in what was left of his home. And Curtis Cook discovered his high school football photo in the remains of his family's house. In a strange twist, the photo had also survived the 1999 Moore tornado, which destroyed his family's previous house.

For every story of loss and devastation, there were dozens more of hope and survival—like Shayla Taylor's story. She was in labor at the Moore Medical Center as the twister barreled straight for the hospital. The tornado badly damaged her hospital room, but nurses were able to get her into a better protected operating room just in time to deliver her son, Braeden Immanuel. The Oklahoma City area had made it through another EF5 tornado.

Shayla Taylor gave birth to her son during the tornado.

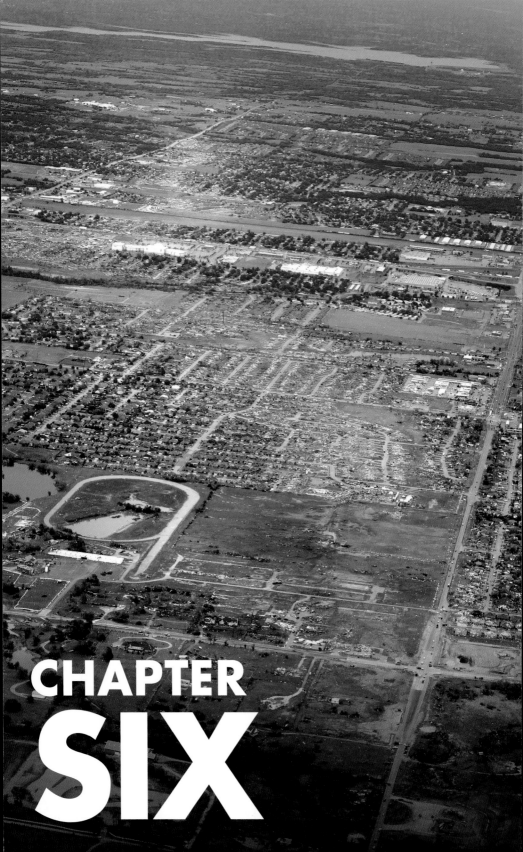

CHAPTER
SIX

IN THE BULL'S-EYE

Tornadoes can and have formed on almost every continent of the world. Yet the United States is the country most likely to be hit by tornadoes, getting approximately 1,200 of them each year. Canada is a very distant second, with 100 tornadoes annually. Approximately 95 percent of tornadoes in the United States are below an EF3. Less than 1 percent are EF5 tornadoes.[1] If the United States is a tornado target, then Tornado Alley is in the bull's-eye of that target. And Oklahoma is in the dead center of that bull's-eye.

By September 2013, there were 72 tornado touchdowns in Oklahoma for the year. Fifty-six of them were in May.[2] Most were EF0 or EF1 tornadoes. However, one EF4 and two EF5s did hit the state during the 2013 season. In just a 15-year period, Moore was hit by three major tornadoes, two of them EF5s.

The rare EF5 tornado of May 20 was the first of two to hit Oklahoma in 2013, causing major damage to the state.

Struck Three Times

It is rare for the same town to be hit by two major tornadoes. Moore has been hit not twice, but three times. On May 3, 1999, dozens of twisters raged across the Great Plains. A huge EF5 tornado blew through the center of Moore, killing 40 people and injuring hundreds more.[3] Then in 2003, another tornado—this one an EF3 or EF4—struck Moore. Although no one was killed, the tornado caused hundreds of millions of dollars of damage. It destroyed homes and businesses.

When considering not just Moore, but the Oklahoma City area as a whole, the region has long been fertile ground for tornadoes. Between 1890 and 2012, there were reports of nearly 150 tornadoes.[6] That means more than one tornado hits this single metropolitan area each year. On 25 different occasions, two or more tornadoes have struck on the same day.

Why has the Oklahoma City area, and especially Moore, experienced so many tornadoes? Sitting in the middle of Tornado Alley, Oklahoma City is a prime

DEADLIEST TORNADOES IN US HISTORY

Tornadoes are not measured only by their monetary cost. Even more important is the number of human lives they take. Here are some of the deadliest tornadoes to strike US soil since meteorologists began tracking these storms.

- Natchez, Mississippi, on May 7, 1840
  This tornado blew down the Mississippi River. More than 300 people died along both the Mississippi and Louisiana sides of the river.[7]

- Tri-State Tornado, on March 18, 1925
  On its 219-mile (352-km) run through Missouri, Illinois, and Indiana, this EF5 tornado killed nearly 700 people and caused more than 2,000 injuries. In Murphysboro,

Illinois, alone, 234 people were killed.[8]

- Tupelo, Mississippi, and Gainesville, Georgia, on April 5–6, 1936
  The death toll from this two-day tornado outbreak reached nearly 500.[9]

- Woodward, Oklahoma, on April 9, 1947
  This funnel cloud was part of a larger system that also affected Kansas and Texas. The small town of Woodward in the northwest corner of Oklahoma was hardest hit, with 107 of the storm's 181 total deaths. More than 100 city blocks in Woodward were leveled, and more than 1,000 homes and businesses were destroyed.[10]

Supercell Thunderstorm

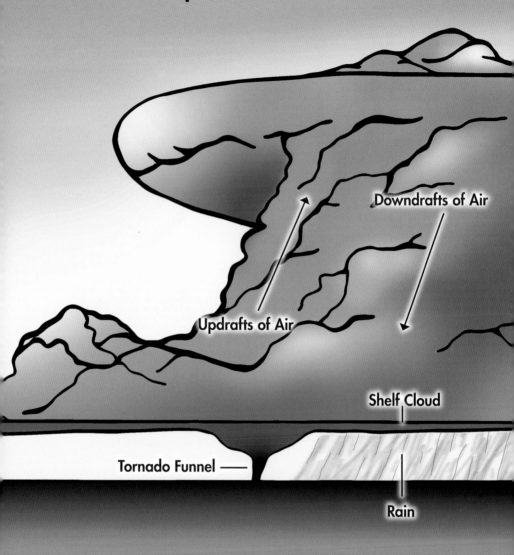

Downdrafts of Air

Updrafts of Air

Shelf Cloud

Tornado Funnel —

Rain

location for supercell thunderstorms to form. These strong storms are likely to give birth to twisters.

Yet it is still very rare for so many strong tornadoes to follow the same path. More likely, the city of Moore has suffered from a string of bad luck. The three tornadoes to hit Moore were probably just coincidence, meteorologists say. "If I gave you 1,000 darts and blindfolded you, and you threw the darts, some would cluster together," said Robin Tanamachi, a researcher at the National Severe Storms Laboratory in Norman. "That's, I think, what's happening here. It's a random statistical fluke. Moore has been unlucky."[11]

All three of the major tornadoes to strike Moore followed a very similar path. As a result, many of the same people were hit by a major tornado more than once. Hundreds of people in Moore

SUPERCELL THUNDERSTORMS

There are three types of thunderstorms. Single cell storms usually take place in the summertime. They can produce thunder and lightning, but they usually are not severe. Multicell thunderstorms are separate storms that merge together into one big storm. The strongest storms are in the middle of the cloud cluster.

The most powerful storms are supercell thunderstorms. They contain rotating updrafts of air, which are caused by wind shear— changes in wind speed and direction at various heights of the atmosphere. Supercells are the type of storms that produce hail, damaging winds, and tornadoes.

lost everything they had during the 1999 tornado. Many of them rebuilt, only to lose their homes again.

"I can't think of any other city of that size in the country that's had three hits of this magnitude within that time span," said meteorologist and writer Robert Henson. "That's the big part of what made this so additionally horrible. Any city hit by this [strong of a tornado] is awful, but the fact that they rebuilt twice before is just terrible."[12]

Helping Each Other

The ordeal of seeing their town leveled by a twister could have made people angry and bitter. But in Moore, tornadoes have brought out the best in people.

As soon as they emerged from their shelters on May 20, 2013, neighbors ran to help each other. Moore's

The city of Moore was badly damaged by both the
1999 tornado, *left*, and the 2013 tornado, *right*.

Jim Stubblefield raises a torn flag he found as he helped his sister sort through what remained of her home.

residents dug through the rubble to find those who had been injured and to salvage family mementos from destroyed homes. Hundreds of people showed up to clear debris from Moore's biggest cemetery so the town could hold its annual Memorial Day services on May 27.

CHAPTER
SEVEN

PROTECTION FROM THE STORM

The people of Moore had approximately 16 minutes to prepare for the May 20, 2013, tornado after the tornado emergency warning. That might not sound like much time, but compared to lead times just a few decades ago, tornado warnings have improved a great deal.

Advanced Warning

Fifteen years ago, weather forecasters could predict only one day in advance that severe, tornado-producing storms were about to form. Today they can start preparing residents for tornadoes a week in advance. That advance warning is mainly thanks to better radar and computer systems.

Tornado warning times have improved, too. In the 1970s, people who were in the path of a tornado had just three minutes to prepare. By the 1980s, the

High-tech tools help meteorologists better predict the formation of tornadoes.

MODERN TORNADO WARNING

The modern tornado warning system was born in 1948. On March 20 of that year, a tornado struck Tinker Air Force Base in Oklahoma City without any warning. The twister toppled military planes and left millions of dollars of damage.

Forecasters at the base began looking at weather charts to see if they could find patterns indicating a tornado was about to form. On March 25, two forecasters noticed the day's weather charts looked almost the same as the March 20 weather charts. They issued their first tornado warning. Just after 6:00 p.m., a tornado made a direct hit on the base. The tornado warning was successful.

warning time had increased to five minutes. The average lead time between a tornado warning and a strike today is 13 minutes, according to NOAA. Forecasters issue warnings by looking at Doppler radar images showing air rotation. They also use visual sightings of funnels with debris reported by volunteer storm spotters. These images and visual cues are the clearest signs of a tornado.

Tornado warning lead times are so important because they give people the chance to seek cover. The more time people have to find shelter, the more lives are saved. The Tri-State Tornado struck Missouri, Illinois, and Indiana in 1925—decades before modern weather forecasting and tornado warnings became available. It killed 695 people and injured more than 2,000 others.[1]

"Advanced notice is very important," said John Trostel, director of the Severe Storms Research Center at the Georgia Tech Research Institute in Atlanta, Georgia. "That is why, even with such a massive scale of destruction [in the Moore tornado], we are seeing tens of casualties instead of hundreds."[2]

HISTORY OF TORNADO WARNING SYSTEMS

Before the 1800s, when a tornado was about to hit a town, the people who lived there had no way of knowing. In the 1880s, scientists started to learn which conditions triggered tornadoes. US Army Signal Corps Sergeant John P. Finley, who headed tornado investigation, developed a list of 15 rules to be used in weather forecasting. Tornado forecasting was included in his list, which was published in 1888.

In 1887, just as tornado warnings were moving forward, there was a setback. The US government banned the use of the word *tornado* in weather forecasting. The government was concerned issuing warnings would cause people to panic and therefore do more harm than good. That ban was finally lifted in 1938.

In the 1950s, once radar had been invented, it helped meteorologists spot tornadoes while the storms were still in the sky. Meteorologists used television and radio programs to send out tornado warnings to the public. In the 1970s, tornado sirens were built in areas often hit with twisters.

Today, meteorologists have radar systems and computers to pinpoint tornadoes before they hit. When a tornado is about to form, the NWS can immediately warn the people in its path in many ways, including the Internet, cell phones, tornado sirens, weather radios, and television news programs.

A destroyed siren sits in the rubble after the May 20 Moore tornado.

Oklahoma City's Warning Systems

The people of Oklahoma know very well the importance
of tornado warnings. After the 1999 EF5 tornado,
Oklahoma City replaced its old tornado warning system
that had been used for decades. The city's modern
network included 182 sirens—36 of them in Moore
alone. The city also started a "code red" notification
system. It calls and sends out e-mail and text messages
to homes in the path of the storm. This system was not
activated when the May 2013 tornadoes hit because the

city's government officials believed the sirens would be a more effective way to alert residents.

In 2001, Moore was one of the first cities in the country to be deemed "StormReady" by the NWS. StormReady means the city monitors weather constantly, has a 24-hour emergency operations center, holds emergency exercises to prepare residents for a tornado, and sends out weather warnings in several different ways, such as by phone and e-mail.

In the future, forecasters hope they can issue warnings with a one-hour lead time, rather than minutes. They will send out these warnings ahead of a storm, based on weather patterns and supercell thunderstorm forecasts, instead of once the storms have already formed.

Scientists are improving storm warnings by finding out as much as they can about how tornadoes form. One way they learn this information is by putting scientific instruments directly in the path of a tornado. When the winds blow over them, the instruments measure wind speeds, pressure, and other information from right inside the tornado.

Scientists also use computers and modeling software to predict when and where severe storms will form.

These tools have become more accurate over the years. "We've got a long way to go, but I think we're making steady progress," said Christopher Karstens, a research scientist with the National Severe Storms Laboratory in Norman.[3] The goal is to predict exactly which supercell thunderstorms will give birth to tornadoes and precisely where those tornadoes will hit.

Oklahoma's Shelters

It might seem obvious an area sitting in the middle of Tornado Alley would have safe rooms and storm shelters in every home, business, and school. Yet only 2.5 percent of homes in Oklahoma City have these shelters. Moore's city municipal code does not require homeowners to build shelters. There are no community storm shelters in Moore. And many of the older schools, including Plaza Towers Elementary School, do not have shelters.

Oklahoma has made some changes for the better in recent years. Kelley Elementary School in Moore, which was destroyed during the 1999 tornado, was rebuilt with stronger, reinforced walls to withstand tornado-force winds. But even after that storm, Oklahoma did not make it a requirement for all new schools and homes to have storm shelters.

Building safe rooms and storm shelters is harder than it might seem. "It sounds really easy to say every school should have a safe room. It's much more complicated," said Angie Besendorfer, an assistant school superintendent in Joplin, Missouri, which was hit by an EF5 tornado in 2011. "There is not a one-size-fits-all solution."[4]

One of the biggest barriers to building tornado shelters is cost. A home shelter measuring just eight by eight feet (2.4 by 2.4 m) can cost $8,000 or more

STORM SHELTERS

Many people in areas frequently hit by tornadoes, such as Oklahoma, build safe rooms and storm shelters inside or next to their homes. These structures are either dug underneath the ground or are built strong enough to withstand tornado-force winds and flying debris. They are often made from storm-resistant materials, such as reinforced concrete or steel.

Metal storm shelters, although expensive, are one safety option for Oklahomans who live in tornado-prone areas.

to build. Building safe rooms in schools can cost up to $1 million per project. That is why most shelters are built only in new schools.

Another problem for building storm shelters in Oklahoma is the land. The soil there contains red clay. When that soil gets wet, it expands. When it dries, it contracts. Any structures built underground become very unstable, which means a house with a basement or storm shelter risks cracking.

After May 2013, the Oklahoma state government started taking a more serious look at changing policies to require and fund more storm shelters. Some lawmakers even started a nonprofit organization to raise money for tornado-safe buildings. Moore Mayor Glen Lewis announced he would propose an ordinance requiring every new home be built with a storm shelter. Moore's city council also discussed constructing homes and other structures using stronger materials to better withstand storms. Before Oklahoma lawmakers had a chance to make any decisions, another tornado was upon the Oklahoma City area.

CHAPTER
EIGHT

MORE TORNADOES

After the May 20 tornado, it seemed the people in Oklahoma City had lived through the worst weather they could endure. But the storm season was not over yet.

On the evening of May 31, just 11 days after the tornado wiped out much of Moore, the skies over the Oklahoma City area again grew dark. Another storm of epic proportions was about to hit.

Torrential rain fell from the skies, flooding roads and rivers. Baseball-sized hail turned into dangerous projectiles. The same storm system spawned heavy rains and tornadoes throughout Missouri and Illinois. More than a dozen tornadoes were reported—eight of them in central Oklahoma.

At approximately 6:00 p.m., a supercell thunderstorm formed over the Oklahoma City area. It swept toward El Reno, a town 25 miles (40 km) west of Oklahoma City. Tornado sirens began blaring. Just

The sky darkened once again in Oklahoma on May 31, 2013.

as people in the El Reno area were driving home from work, a tornado dropped from the clouds.

Caught in Rush Hour

It was the worst possible time for a tornado to hit. The roadways around El Reno were choked with rush hour traffic. Instead of seeking shelter where they were, as people are warned to do in a tornado, many people tried to outrun the storm. Interstate 40, the main roadway in the El Reno area, was packed with cars and trucks. The traffic was so heavy no cars could move. The tornado barreled straight for the stranded motorists.

Even drivers on less crowded roads were in trouble. With the dark storm clouds overhead, it was impossible to see the tornado's exact location. "Some tornadoes are wrapped in rain, so it's basically impossible to see, which is extremely dangerous," said NWS meteorologist Bruce Thoren. "Somebody driving along really not familiar with what's going on can basically drive into it."[1]

In addition to the tornado, heavy rains flooded many roads. And the storm's high winds tore down power lines, leaving the ground littered with live wires, making driving even more perilous. As drivers fled from the unseen tornado, they panicked. The memory of the previous tornado's destruction was still fresh in everyone's minds. "I think we are still a little shaken by what happened in Moore," said Oklahoma City Mayor Mick Cornett. "We are still burying children and victims, so our emotions are still strong."[2]

"It was chaos. People were going southbound in the northbound lanes. Everybody was running for their lives," said local resident Terri Black.[3] People were driving on the shoulders of the road and on the grass, trying to get away. The frightened motorists included Amy Sharp, who, just a week earlier, had pulled her fourth grader from Plaza Towers Elementary School as a tornado sped toward Moore.

This time the tornado slammed right into Interstate 40, lifting cars and semitrailer trucks into the

STAY PUT OR DRIVE AWAY?

Weather warnings from local television stations are critical when a tornado is approaching. But during the El Reno storm, one television meteorologist gave advice many people questioned afterward.

While broadcasting reports of the storm, KFOR chief meteorologist Mike Morgan first told viewers to get into a storm cellar or other underground shelter. But then he said, "If you can leave South Oklahoma City and go south do it now." His advice was one of the reasons roads were clogged with traffic when the tornado hit. Some people called Morgan's advice "irresponsible."[4]

A semitrailer was knocked to its side on Interstate 40 on May 31, 2013.

air. One SUV with a family inside was sucked into the tornado's vortex. A mother and her baby who were inside the SUV were killed.

Other drivers who experienced the tornado's power lived to tell the story. "My car was actually lifted off the road and then set back down," Terri Black said. "The trees were leaning literally to the ground. The rain was coming down horizontally in front of my car. Big blue trash cans were being tossed around like a piece of paper in the wind."[5]

What made the storm even deadlier was its unusual path. "It also had a very chaotic movement, moving several different directions over the course of its life that made it difficult to predict where it was heading next," said David Andra, meteorologist in charge with the NWS in Norman. "And if you're in the path, it made it difficult to get out of the way."[6]

Death and Destruction in El Reno

The El Reno tornado was the largest ever recorded, at 2.6 miles (4.2 km) across. That is wider than the entire island of Manhattan, New York. It was like two of the May 20 tornadoes side by side. The El Reno tornado even beat the previous world record for tornado width, which had been held by a 2.5-mile- (4 km) wide tornado that hit Hallam, Nebraska, on May 22, 2004.

With winds of nearly 300 miles per hour (483 kmh), the EF3 El Reno tornado was deadly. It killed 18 people and injured 115 more.[7] Meteorologists said the death toll could have been even higher if the storm hit closer to Oklahoma City instead of in the more rural El Reno area. "The impacts were horrible of what happened, where it hit and what happened to people and structures," said meteorologist Rick Smith. "But had it gone through the very densely populated areas, this would have been . . . I don't even want to imagine what it would have been."[8]

The same storm dumped approximately eight inches (20 cm) of rain on the Oklahoma City area. Roads flooded, and the Oklahoma River overflowed. The storm damage was so severe Governor Mary Fallin declared a state of emergency in 41 Oklahoma counties.

Three Storm Chasers Die

Among the victims of the El Reno tornado were three highly experienced storm chasers—Tim Samaras, his

Parts of the Oklahoma City area flooded after the tornadoes passed.

chasing partner Carl Young, and his son Paul Samaras. The trio was featured on the Discovery Channel show *Storm Chasers*. They were killed when the El Reno tornado took an unexpected turn and crushed their

STORM CHASING—A DANGEROUS BUSINESS

Storm chasers do not hide from storms—they run toward them. Their goal is to get footage of the twister and collect data about the storm. They use this information to learn more about tornadoes and issue more accurate storm warnings.

"A lot of these individuals have dedicated many years of their lives to going out and assisting and tracking storms, and getting footage and putting themselves in harm's way so they can educate the public to the destructive power of these storms," said Canadian County, Oklahoma, Undersheriff Chris West.[9]

Storm chasers such as Tim Samaras, Paul Samaras, and Carl Young, who died in the May 31 tornado, were scientists. Scientist storm chasers chase tornadoes to collect data and are always very careful not to drive too close to storms.

Not everyone is as careful, however. Thrill seekers chase storms purely for the excitement—or money. Thanks to reality television shows and YouTube clips, more people than ever before are fascinated by storm chasing and want to try it out. Their goal is not to learn about tornadoes but to capture the most dramatic video. One close-up clip of a tornado can earn storm chasers hundreds of dollars.

There can be hundreds of inexperienced storm chasers on the Oklahoma roads during any given tornado outbreak. And that makes for a very risky situation. "There are more and more people out there on the road. Many of them should not be," according to veteran Oklahoma storm chaser Lanny Dean. "We're talking about individuals who are not experienced and who have no clue what they're doing."[10]

white pickup truck. Tim Samaras was found still inside the truck with his seatbelt on. Carl Young and Paul Samaras were thrown from the truck.

These storm chasers were not hotshots looking for a thrill. Tim Samaras was a scientist who had hunted tornadoes for 20 years. He truly loved storm chasing and was willing to take on the danger to learn more about the power of these storms. Samaras founded the Tactical Weather Instrumented Sampling in Tornadoes Experiment, a project to help meteorologists learn more about twisters and increase warning lead times to protect the public.

"This thing is really shaking up everyone in the chasing community," said Doug Kiesling, a cameraman who also chases tornadoes. "We knew this day would happen someday, but nobody would imagine that it would happen to Tim. Tim was one of the safest people to go out there. . . . He's had close calls, but he's always had an escape route."[11]

Another experienced storm chaser had a very close call during the El Reno tornado. Mike Bettes of the Weather Channel was following the storm when the tornado suddenly picked up his truck and threw it 200 yards (183 m). Bettes and the other two members

Storm chasers Carl Young, *left*, and Tim Samaras, *right*, died during the May 31 storm.

of his crew escaped with only minor injuries, but it was a terrifying experience. "I saw people in my life, I saw their faces flash right in front of me. And it just seemed for a moment, everything was in slow motion, especially when we were floating," he said[12]

Experts say the death of three storm chasers might change the way meteorologists track tornadoes in the future. "I think there will be some [storm chasers] who will step back and say: 'Am I really doing something safe here?'" said Michael Armstrong, a meteorologist at KWTV in Oklahoma City.[13]

Storm chasers might change their approach after this tragic loss, but they likely will not stop studying tornadoes. The information they learn each time they go out in a field during a severe storm could one day save countless lives.

CHAPTER
NINE

AFTER THE DISASTER

After the tornado, before-and-after aerial images of Moore were posted on the Internet. In the before photo there are neat rows of houses. The same photo taken after the storm shows empty spaces where those homes used to be. All that was left were piles of debris and the outlines of where houses once stood. Other aerial photos show what little remained of Plaza Towers Elementary School after the tornado.

In addition to tearing down houses, the tornado destroyed businesses and important services in Moore, including the community hospital. Phone and power lines were down, making it hard for people who still had a house to live in it. Chris Drevecky and Tiffany Knox's home was standing after the tornado, but it was badly damaged. They had no electricity or drinking water, which was hard on Knox, who was pregnant. The couple had nowhere to go.

A view of Moore's Medical Center shows cars that had been tossed against the building, along with other damage.

Cleaning Up

As soon as rescue efforts to find anyone trapped from the tornado were done, recovery operations began. Crews had to restore basic services, such as water and power, to the people of Moore. Utility crews were out fixing their equipment. Construction crews came out to move the debris. And people walked the streets pulling wagons. They were returning to their destroyed homes to retrieve any possessions they could find.

One of the biggest challenges was picking up the piles of debris lying all over the area. The tornado had tossed buildings into the air, ripped them to shreds, and then deposited them yards—or even miles—from where they once stood. Three weeks after the tornado, 23,000 short tons (20,865 metric tons) of debris had been picked up.

Friends and family members remove what remained of
a piano from the pile of a home's wreckage.

LOST IN THE STORM

When the tornado tore through neighborhoods in Moore, it did more than destroy homes. It also took away mementos. People's photographs of weddings, graduations, and newborn babies were scattered in the wind. Precious family mementos were lost or destroyed.

Yet many people found their possessions, sometimes in unexpected places. A cherished photograph of Randy Sanders' family was discovered in a backyard 120 miles (193 km) away. Other photos, letters, and personal items were found up to 250 miles (402 km) from Moore. A Facebook page called "May 2013 Oklahoma Tornado Doc & Photo Recovery Page" was started to help reunite people with their lost belongings.

Any severely damaged buildings had to be bulldozed.

While they picked up what was left of their homes and possessions, the people of Moore needed to recover emotionally. Grief counselors were on hand to help residents mourn for the friends and family they had lost. Teachers got together to share their experiences during the storm and to recount how they protected the children in their care.

Teams of volunteers came from around the country, some traveling hundreds of miles to help. Lucas Sjaarda came from Michigan with a group of 30 people from his church. "I can't believe it, if this was my home, I wouldn't know what to do," he said.[2]

Residents who had lost everything found help at American Red Cross centers and local church shelters. There they were offered beds to sleep in, as well as food, clean drinking water, and clothing.

A memorial service to the storm's victims was held. And outside Plaza Towers Elementary School, people left piles of stuffed animals and messages of hope and remembrance for the lost children.

Declared Disaster Areas

After the storms, officials in Oklahoma tallied the damage. Approximately 12,000 homes had been destroyed or damaged, plus hundreds of businesses. The total cost of the storm was estimated at $2 billion.[3]

President Barack Obama declared Oklahoma City a major disaster area. This allowed residents to file for government assistance, which would give them money to pay for their lost homes and businesses. The president vowed government assistance would continue until the town was able to recover. President Obama said, "The people of Moore should know that their country will remain on the ground for them, beside them, for as long as it takes for their homes and schools to rebuild."[4]

As he mourned the tornado losses, President Obama also looked hopefully ahead. "There are empty spaces where there used to be living rooms, and bedrooms, and classrooms, and, in time, we're going to need to refill those spaces with love and laughter and community," he said in a speech.[5]

Money to Help Storm Victims

A month after the storm hit, the American Red Cross had already received $26 million in donations for the Oklahoma tornado victims. The Federal Emergency Management Agency (FEMA), a government agency

HURRICANE SANDY VICTIMS HELP

Students from East Rockaway High School in Long Island, New York, know something about storms. In 2012, Hurricane Sandy blew through their town, destroying parts of their school. Eventually their high school was rebuilt and their lives returned to normal.

A year later, those same students learned a tornado destroyed the high school in Moore, Oklahoma. They wanted to help their fellow students. They organized a basketball tournament, bake sale, car wash, and other fund-raisers to raise money for Oklahoma tornado victims. "I think it's important to pay it forward because this is how we are, the kind of town we are," said East Rockaway High School eleventh grader Tiffini Parente. "We know what it feels like to be out of our town for six months, we know what it feels like to not have a home."[6] By June 15, the East Rockaway students had raised almost $8,000 for tornado relief.

that helps with disaster recovery, approved more than $8 million for people affected by the storm.

Even though many homeowners had insurance, they needed extra money to get their lives back to normal. Well-known celebrities chipped in to help. Country singer Blake Shelton, who is from Oklahoma, organized a benefit concert. On May 29, NBC aired his special, *Healing in the Heartland: Relief Benefit Concert*, which was held at Oklahoma City's Chesapeake Energy Arena. Country stars Miranda Lambert, Reba McEntire, and Vince Gill performed. The concert raised more than $6 million for the United Way of Central Oklahoma May Tornadoes Relief Fund.

Looting after the Storms

Disasters can bring out the best and the worst in people. After the tornado struck Moore, people came to the town from all over the country to offer their help.

Yet other people tried to take advantage of the situation. Looters quickly moved into the destroyed areas, trying to steal what they could. Families returning to see what was left of their homes found strangers picking through the rubble. Some looters were even more brazen. "The houses are still standing

Michael Tackett helped clean up the debris of his friend's home in Moore.

and looters are kicking in doors and taking TVs and appliances," said Jon Fisher, whose home was destroyed in the storm. "They arrested two guys in my neighborhood the night of the tornado who were carrying out a love seat and couch."[7] Thieves were also caught stealing pipes and scrap metal.

Police officers set up around-the-clock watches in tornado-hit neighborhoods. They checked the identification of everyone entering the areas to make sure they lived there. By mid-June, police had arrested 17 people for looting.

The Pledge to Rebuild

Just days after the tornado tore apart their town, Moore residents vowed to start over, even though they knew it would not be easy. "Rebuilding will take time because things are just gone. You have a cement slab where a house once was and nothing else, and this goes on for blocks. It's a helpless feeling, but we are going to stay put," said Lesley Bell, a supervisor in the Moore school district.[8]

Mayor Glenn Lewis was hopeful it would take only about two years to rebuild most of the homes lost in Moore. "We've already started printing the street signs," he said just one day after the tornado. "It took 61 days to clean up after the 1999 tornado. We had a lot of help then. We've got a lot of help now."[9]

Moore announced plans to rebuild Briarwood and Plaza Towers Elementary schools exactly where they once stood. School superintendent Susan Pierce said it was important to put the schools where they were to get the children's lives back to normal. "We think it's essential for the kids and the community to come back strong at the same location," she said. Not everyone agreed with the plan, however. "They can rebuild, but not in the same exact spot. People died there," said Antonio Garcia, a sixth grader who survived the storm at Plaza Towers Elementary School.[10] Residents also wanted to make sure the schools were built stronger or with safe rooms so the children would be protected if other tornadoes were to strike.

Coming Back Stronger

Oklahomans have survived many tragedies. In the 1930s, there was the dust bowl, a drought so severe it turned soil to dust and destroyed all the crops. In 1995, Timothy McVeigh bombed the Alfred P. Murrah Federal Building in Oklahoma City, killing 168 people.

And then, the region was hit by a string of tornadoes, some of which wiped out entire towns.

Yet each disaster brought the people of Oklahoma together. "I'm pretty devastated that this has happened, but overall I think it has brought this community closer and made us all think never to take our lives for granted because you truly never know when it's your last day," said 14-year-old Marcella Corrales, a high-school student in Moore.[11]

Many people who live outside of Oklahoma wondered why anyone would want to stay in a town where so many tornadoes have hit. "Why do we stay here? We're used to this, just like Californians are used to earthquakes," said elementary schoolteacher Pam Lewis, who is married to Moore's Mayor Glenn Lewis. "We love this place, and we will rebuild. Our whole life is here."[12]

FINDING LOST PETS

Once the storm passed, crews of rescuers sifted through the rubble, searching for human survivors. Many pets were also lost.

Emily Garman, coowner of a local Web design company, created the Web site OKCLostPets.com to help residents find their pets. The local Home Depot set up an animal location command center. Thanks to these efforts, many pets were reunited with their owners.

TIMELINE

1840
On May 7, a tornado blows down the Mississippi River, killing more than 300 people in Mississippi and Louisiana.

1880s
Scientists learn which conditions trigger tornadoes.

1887
The US government bans the use of the word *tornado* in weather warnings. The ban is eventually lifted in 1938.

1896
On May 27, a tornado destroys more than 8,000 buildings and kills more than 250 people in Saint Louis, Missouri.

1925
The Tri-State Tornado strikes Illinois, Indiana, and Missouri on March 18.

1927

A tornado tears a path of destruction through the middle of Saint Louis, Missouri, on September 29.

1936

On April 5–6, a tornado outbreak kills nearly 500 people in Mississippi and Georgia.

1947

The town of Woodward, Oklahoma, loses 107 people and more than 100 city blocks during a twister on April 9.

1948

Tinker Air Force Base in Oklahoma City issues the first official tornado warning on March 25.

1957

A *New York Times* article coins the term *Tornado Alley*.

TIMELINE

1999
An EF5 tornado strikes Moore, Oklahoma, on May 3.

2001
Moore becomes one of the first cities in the country to be called "StormReady" by the National Weather Service (NWS).

2003
An EF3 or EF4 tornado strikes Moore on May 8—the town's second direct hit in four years.

2011
On May 22, a twister tears through the town of Joplin, Missouri.

2013

- On May 20 at 2:40 p.m., the NWS issues tornado warnings for Moore and the Oklahoma City area.
- At 2:56 p.m., the tornado starts to descend from the skies over Newcastle, Oklahoma. It travels toward Moore, gaining strength as it goes.
- At 3:01 p.m., the NWS issues a tornado emergency, the strongest possible warning, for Moore and southern Oklahoma City.
- At 3:16 p.m., the EF5 tornado enters Moore.
- At 3:36 p.m., the tornado lifts up near Lake Stanley Draper.

2013

On May 29, the *Healing in the Heartland* benefit concert airs on NBC to raise money for Oklahoma tornado victims.

2013

On May 31, an EF3 tornado hits El Reno, Oklahoma.

ESSENTIAL FACTS

Date of Event
May 20, 2013, and May 31, 2013

Place of Event
Moore and El Reno, Oklahoma

Key Players
- Rick Smith, National Weather Service meteorologist

- David Andra, National Weather Service lead meteorologist

- Gary England, former chief meteorologist for KWTV News 9, Oklahoma City

- Oklahoma Governor Mary Fallin

Highlights of Event
- An EF5 tornado ripped a 14-mile (22.5 km) path through Moore, Oklahoma, on May 20, 2013, at 3:16 p.m.

- After the storm, the Oklahoma City area began rescue and recovery operations to find people still trapped from the storm and to restore basic services.

- Twenty-four people were killed, including seven students at Plaza Towers Elementary School. Three hundred and seventy-five people were injured, and 12,000 homes were destroyed.

- On May 31, 2013, an EF3 tornado hit El Reno, Oklahoma.

- The El Reno tornado became the largest ever recorded, twice as wide as the May 20 tornado.

- The El Reno tornado killed 18 people, including several experienced storm chasers. It injured 115 others.

Quote

"We saw a funnel cloud emerge over the west side of Oklahoma City metro. This was a worst nightmare for a storm spotter. The tornado grew to a size I had never seen before. Close to a mile wide at times. And it was just so sad because the tornado formed right over the city and I'd never seen anything like it." —*Ben McMillan, storm chaser*

GLOSSARY

downdraft
A downward current of air.

embedded
When an object becomes buried deep inside another object.

fossil fuel
A type of fuel, such as coal, oil, or gas, that comes from the remains of animals and plants that lived millions of years ago.

Fujita scale
A tornado rating system developed by Dr. Theodore Fujita in the early 1970s. It classifies tornadoes based on the damage their winds cause.

humid
Containing a high amount of moisture.

incubator
A controlled environment used to help something grow—such as a premature baby or storm.

jet stream
A fast-moving current of air high above Earth's surface.

loot
To steal things during a war, fire, or other disturbance.

safe room
A room built strongly enough to withstand tornado-force winds.

state of emergency
An official declaration by the government that gives people money and other types of support to help them recover from storms and other disasters.

tornado emergency
A warning from the National Weather Service that means a very severe and strong tornado is headed for an area.

tornado warning
An alert issued by government meteorologists to warn people a tornado has formed or is likely to form.

updraft
An upward movement of air.

ADDITIONAL RESOURCES

Selected Bibliography

Coleman, Timothy A., et al. "The History (And Future) of Tornado Warning Dissemination in the United States." *Bulletin of the American Meteorological Society*. May 2011. Print.

Dennis, Alicia, et al. "Oklahoma Tornado: Braving the Storm." *People*. Time, 3 June 2013. Print.

"Historic Tornado Outbreaks." *Weather Channel*. Weather Channel, n.d. Web.

Romano, Andrew. "When the Sirens Wailed." *Newsweek*. IBT Media, 22 May 2013. Web.

"2013 Oklahoma Tornadoes." *NOAA*. NOAA, 22 June 2013. Web.

Von Drehle, David, et al. "16 Minutes." *Time*. Time, 3 June 2013. Web.

Further Readings

Carson, Mary Kay. *Inside Tornadoes* (Inside Series). New York: Sterling, 2010. Print.

Fradin, Judy, and Dennis Fradin. *Tornado! The Story Behind These Twisting, Turning, Spinning, and Spiraling Storms.* Des Moines, IA: National Geographic Children's, 2011. Print.

Web Sites

To learn more about the 2013 Oklahoma City tornadoes, visit ABDO Publishing Company online at **www.abdopublishing.com**. Web sites about the 2013 Oklahoma City tornadoes are featured on our Book Links page. These links are routinely monitored and updated to provide the most current information available.

Places to Visit

City of Moore, Oklahoma
http://www.cityofmoore.com
Moore is a suburb of Oklahoma City. It has been hit with an unusually high number of tornadoes over the years.

Museum of Science and Industry
5700 S. Lake Shore Drive
Chicago, IL 60637
773-684-1414
http://www.msichicago.org/whats-here/exhibits/science-storms/the-exhibit/tornado/tornado
This Chicago science museum is home to a 40-foot (12 m) tornado simulation.

SOURCE NOTES

Chapter 1. Taking Cover

1. Jeremy Singer-Vine. "How Did "Tornado Alley" Get Its Name?" *Slate*. Slate, 21 May 2013. Web. 23 May 2013.

2. "Tornado and Severe Weather Preparedness." *City of Oklahoma City*. City of Oklahoma City, n.d. Web. 23 June 2013.

3. Jane C. Timm. "Stories of Loss, 'Apocalyptic' Damage, and Courage in Moore, Okla." *MSNBC*. NBC Universal, 21 May 2013. Web. 23 June 2013.

4. Kurt Gwartney. "Massive Tornado Takes Aim at Moore, Oklahoma." *NPR*. NPR, 21 May 2013. Web. 17 Sept. 2013.

5. Mel Bracht. "Oklahoma Tornadoes." *Oklahoman*. Oklahoman, 28 May 2013. Web. 29 June 2013.

6. David Von Drehle, et al. "16 Minutes." *Time*. Time, 3 June 2013. Web. 17 June 2013.

7. Jay Newton-Small. "Wrenching Decisions as Tornado Flattens School." *Time*. Time, 22 May 2013. Web. 17 Sept. 2013.

8. Ibid.

9. Andrew Romano. "When the Sirens Wailed." *Newsweek*. IBT Media, 22 May 2013. Web. 17 June 2013.

10. Alicia Dennis, et al. "Oklahoma Tornado." *People*. Time, 3 June 2013. Print.

11. Christina Ng. "Oklahoma Tornado." *ABC News*. ABC News, 21 May 2013. Web. 23 June 2013.

Chapter 2. The Approaching Storm

1. Tim Layden. "Seeking Shelter." *Sports Illustrated*. Time, 3 June 2013. Web. 17 June 2013.

2. "Doppler Radar." *National Weather Service*. National Oceanic and Atmospheric Administration, n.d. Web. 13 Sept. 2013.

3. "Storm Chaser Describes Watching 'Nightmare Tornado' Form over Moore, Oklahoma—Video 5/20/13." *Freedom's Lighthouse*. Freedom's Lighthouse, 20 May 2013. Web. 11 July 2013.

4. Tim Layden. "Seeking Shelter." *Sports Illustrated*. Time, 3 June 2013. Web. 17 June 2013.

5. Eryn Brown. "Weather Conditions Were Ideal for the Tornado That Slammed Oklahoma." *Chicago Tribune*. Chicago Tribune, 21 May 2013. Web. 16 June 2013.

Chapter 3. Tornado Sirens Wail

1. Michael C. Bender. "Oklahoma Tornado Alert Gave Residents 36 Minutes Warning." *Bloomberg*. Bloomberg, 21 May 2013. Web. 16 June 2013.

2. Carey and Ian Simpson Gillam. "Oklahoma Tornado Victims Astounded at How They Survived." *Courant*. Hartford Courant, 26 May 2013. Web. 16 June 2013.

3. Jonathan Erdman. "Tornado Debris." *Weather Channel*. Weather Channel, 10 March 2012. Web. 14 Aug 2013.

4. Tim Layden. "Seeking Shelter." *Sports Illustrated*. Time, 3 June 2013. Web. 17 June 2013.

5. Michael C. Bender. "Oklahoma Tornado Alert Gave Residents 36 Minutes Warning." *Bloomberg*. Bloomberg, 21 May 2013. Web. 16 June 2013.

6. Jeffrey Kluger. "Prelude to Disaster." *Time*. Time, 21 May 2013. Web. 29 June 2013.

7. "Moore, OK Deadly Tornado from KFOR Live Broadcast." *YouTube*. YouTube, 20 May 2013. Web. 29 June 2013.

Chapter 4. In the Tornado's Path

1. Colin Lecher. "Was the Oklahoma City Tornado the Worst in History?" *Popular Science*. Popular Science, 22 May 2013. Web. 30 June 2013.

2. Chelsea J. Carter, et al. "Crews Shift from Rescue to Recovery." *CNN*. Cable News Network, 21 May 2013. Web. 30 June 2013.

3. Andrew Romano. "When the Sirens Wailed." *Newsweek*. IBT Media, 22 May 2013. Web. 17 June 2013.

4. Sean Murphy. "Tornadoes Touch Down in Oklahoma, Arkansas." *Yahoo! News*. Associated Press, 31 May 2013. Web. 1 July 2013.

5. Alicia Dennis, et al. "Oklahoma Tornado." *People*. Time, 3 June 2013. Print.

6. Associated Press. "Oklahoma Insurance Department: Moore Tornado Damage Cost May Top $2 Billion." *KJRH.com*. Scripps, 22 May 2013. Web. 14 Sept. 2013.

7. Jon Erdman and Nick Wiltgen. "Billions in Damage: Costliest Tornadoes in U.S. History." *Weather Channel*. Weather Channel, 23 May 2013. Web. 30 June 2013.

8. Ibid.

9. Ibid.

10. David Zucchino and Hailey Branson-Potts. "Fear Followed Oklahoma Tornado but There Are Glimmers of Optimism." *Los Angeles Times*. Los Angeles Times, 22 May 2013. Web. 13 Sept. 2013.

11. Andrew Romano. "When the Sirens Wailed." *Newsweek*. IBT Media, 22 May 2013. Web. 17 June 2013.

12. Becky Evans. "There Were Horses and Stuff Flying Around Everywhere." *Daily Mail*. Associated Newspapers, 21 May 2013. Web. 13 Sept. 2013.

Chapter 5. After the Storm

1. David Von Drehle, et al. "16 Minutes." *Time*. Time, 3 June 2013. Web. 17 June 2013.

2. Alicia Dennis, et al. "Oklahoma Tornado." *People*. Time, 3 June 2013. Print.

3. David Zucchino. "Fear Followed Oklahoma Tornado but There Are Glimmers of Optimism." *Chicago Tribune*. Chicago Tribune, 22 May 2013. Web. 16 June 2013.

4. Cindy Carcamo and Ashley Powers. "Storm Cellar Drama." *Los Angeles Times*. Los Angeles Times, 21 May 2013. Web. 2 July 2013.

5. Philip Sherwell. "Oklahoma Tornado." *Telegraph*. Telegraph Media Group, 22 May 2013. Web. 11 July 2013.

6. Lydia Warren, et al. "I Can't Explain My Anger and Sadness." *The Daily Mail*. Associated Newspapers, 20 May 2013. Web. 16 June 2013.

7. Mark Strassman. "Dad Mourns Death of Daughter Killed at Elementary School in Moore." *CBS News*. CBS Interactive, 21 May, 2013. Web. 2 July 2013.

8. Ashley Fantz. "Families Remember Oklahoma Tornado Victims." *CNN*. Cable News Network, 30 May 2013. Web. 2 July 2013.

9. "Moore Residents Hold Services for Animals Lost in Central Oklahoma Tornadoes." *KJRH.com*. Scripps, 16 June 2013. Web. 3 July 2013.

10. Rene Marsh, et al. "One Week Later." *CNN*. Cable News Network, 28 May 2013. Web. 2 July 2013.

SOURCE NOTES CONTINUED

11. Dana Hertneky. "Family Finds Pet Cat Alive Inside Wall of Destroyed Home in Moore." *9 News*. Multimedia Holdings, 11 June 2013. Web. 16 June 2013.

Chapter 6. In the Bull's-Eye

1. "U.S. Tornado Climatology." *NOAA*. National Oceanic and Atmospheric Administration, 17 May 2013. Web. 3 July 2013.

2. "2013 Oklahoma Tornadoes." *NOAA*. National Oceanic and Atmospheric Administration, 22 June 2013. Web. 3 July 2013.

3. John Metcalfe. "Moore, Oklahoma, Has an Uncanny History of Violent Tornadoes." *Atlantic Cities*. Atlantic Monthly, 21 May 2013. Web. 7 July 2013.

4. Ker Than. "Why Is Oklahoma So Tornado Vexed?" *National Geographic*. National Geographic, 1 June 2013. Web. 7 July 2013.

5. Olga Khazan. "Where Else Do Tornadoes Strike?" *Atlantic*. Atlantic Monthly, 21 May 2013. Web. 7 July 2013.

6. Jon Erdman. "Notorious Moore, Oklahoma City Tornado History." *Weather Channel*. Weather Channel, 1 June 2013. Web. 7 July 2013.

7. "Historic Tornado Outbreaks." *Weather Channel*. Weather Channel, n.d. Web. 8 July 2013.

8. "NOAA/NWS 1925 Tri-State Tornado Web Site—Startling Statistics." *NOAA*. National Oceanic and Atmospheric Administration, 2 Mar. 2010. Web. 8 July 2013.

9. "Historic Tornado Outbreaks." *Weather Channel*. Weather Channel, n.d. Web. 8 July 2013.

10. Tim Newcomb. "10 Deadliest Tornadoes in U.S. History." *Time*. Time, 21 May 2013. Web. 8 July 2013.

11. Eryn Brown. "Weather Conditions Were Ideal for the Tornado That Slammed Oklahoma." *Chicago Tribune*. Chicago Tribune, 21 May 2013. Web. 16 June 2013.

12. John Metcalfe. "Moore, Oklahoma, Has an Uncanny History of Violent Tornadoes." *Atlantic Cities*. Atlantic Monthly, 21 May 2013. Web. 7 July 2013.

13. "Massive Okla. Tornado Had Windspeed Up to 200 mph." *CBS News*. CBS Interactive, 20 May 2013. Web. 30 June 2013.

14. John Metcalfe. "Moore, Oklahoma, Has an Uncanny History of Violent Tornadoes." *Atlantic Cities*. Atlantic Monthly, 21 May 2013. Web. 13 Sept. 2013.

15. Ed Arnold. "Cost of Moore, Okla. Tornado Estimated at $2B." *Memphis Business Journal*. American City Business Journals, 22 May 2013. Web. 30 June 2013.

Chapter 7. Protection from the Storm

1. "NOAA/NWS 1925 Tri-State Tornado Web Site—Startling Statistics." *NOAA*. National Oceanic and Atmospheric Administration, 2 Mar. 2010. Web. 14 Sept. 2013.

2. Michael C. Bender. "Oklahoma Tornado Alert Gave Residents 36 Minutes Warning." *Bloomberg*. Bloomberg, 21 May 2013. Web. 16 June 2013.

3. Ker Than. "Why Is Oklahoma So Tornado Vexed?" *National Geographic*. National Geographic, 1 June 2013. Web. 7 July 2013.

4. Nirvi Shah, et al. "Okla. Tornado Renews Debate on Storm Safety." *Education Week*. Editorial Projects in Education, 5 June 2013. Print.

Chapter 8. More Tornadoes

1. "At Least Nine Dead after Deadly Tornadoes Hit Oklahoma City Region." *FOX News*. Fox News, 1 June 2013. Web. 16 June 2013.

2. Heide Brandes. "Death Toll Rises to Nine from Oklahoma Tornadoes." *Reuters*. Thomson Reuters, 1 June 2013. Web. 16 June 2013.

3. Nolan Clay and Andrew Knittle. "Oklahoma Tornadoes." *Oklahoman*. NewsOK, 2 June 2013. Web. 9 July 2013.

4. Alice Mannette. "Mike Morgan, KFOR Meteorologist Vilified for Advice During Oklahoma Tornado." *Huffington Post*. Huffington Post, 6 June 2013. Web. 9 July 2013.

5. Ibid.

6. Bryan Painter and Silas Allen. "El Reno Tornado is 'Super Rare.'" *Oklahoman*. NewsOK, 4 June 2013. Web. 9 July 2013.

7. Ibid.

8. Ibid.

9. Jake Carpenter and Catherine E. Shoichet. "'Unpredictable' Storm in Oklahoma Turned on Three Chasers." *CNN*. Cable News Network, 3 June 2013. Web. 9 July 2013.

10. Sean Murphy. "Storm Chasing Critical, Profitable and Dangerous." *Yahoo! News*. Associated Press, 3 June 2013. Web. 16 June 2013.

11. Jake Carpenter and Catherine E. Shoichet. "'Unpredictable' Storm in Oklahoma Turned on Three Chasers. *CNN*. Cable News Network, 3 June 2013. Web. 9 July 2013.

12. Ibid.

13. Sean Murphy. "Storm Chasing Critical, Profitable and Dangerous." *Yahoo! News*. Associated Press, 3 June 2013. Web. 16 June 2013.

Chapter 9. After the Disaster

1. Heather Hope. "El Reno Mayor Foresees Long Road to Recovery." *News9*. WorldNow and KWTV, 21 June 2013. Web. 15 Aug. 2013.

2. "Okla. Recovering One Month after Deadly Moore Tornado." *KFOR.com*. KFOR, 20 June 2013. Web. 11 July 2013.

3. Heather Hope. "Three Weeks After Deadly Tornado, Progress Made in Moore." *News9*. WorldNow and KWTV, 9 June 2013. Web. 16 June 2013.

4. Lydia Warren, et al. "I Can't Explain My Anger and Sadness." *The Daily Mail*. Associated Newspapers, 20 May 2013. Web. 16 June 2013.

5. Andrew Romano. "When the Sirens Wailed." *Newsweek*. IBT Media, 22 May 2013. Web. 17 June 2013.

6. "Sandy-Struck East Rockaway High School Raises Money for Oklahoma Tornado Victims." *News12*. News12 Interactive, 15 June 2013. Web. 16 June 2013.

7. Heide Brandes. "Scrap Metal, TVs, Love Seats." *NBC News*. NBCNews.com, 13 June 2013. Web. 11 July 2013.

8. Alicia Dennis, et al. "Oklahoma Tornado." *People*. Time, 3 June 2013. Print.

9. "Search for Oklahoma Tornado Survivors Nearly Complete." *Foxnews.com*. Fox News, 22 May 2013. Web. 13 Sept. 2013.

10. Brian Terry. "Oklahoma Schools Destroyed by Tornado to Rebuild." *CBS News*. CBS Interactive, 21 May 2013. Web. 11 July 2013.

11. Alicia Dennis, et al. "Oklahoma Tornado." *People*. Time, 3 June 2013. Print.

12. Michael Walsh. "Oklahoma Tornado Recovery." *Daily News*. NYDailyNews.com, 21 May 2013. Web. 11 July 2013.

INDEX

ABOUT THE AUTHOR

Stephanie Watson is a freelance writer based in Atlanta, Georgia. Over her 20-plus-year career, she has written for television, radio, the Web, and print. Watson has authored more than two dozen books, including *Daniel Radcliffe, Elvis Presley: Rock & Roll's King,* and *Cee Lo Green: Rapper, Singer, & Record Producer.*

ABOUT THE CONSULTANT

Robert J. Trapp is a Professor of Atmospheric Science at Purdue University. He is an expert on convective storms and their attendant hazards, and has written numerous scholarly articles on these and related topics. Trapp also authored the textbook *Mesoscale-Convective Processes in the Atmosphere,* published by Cambridge University Press.